Cecília Eloy Neves

Usability test of the UniClinika RIS Service Module

Cecília Eloy Neves

Usability test of the UniClinika RIS Service Module

Desktop tool for managing diagnostic imaging clinics

ScienciaScripts

Imprint

Cover image: www.ingimage.com

This book is a translation from the original published under ISBN 978-3-330-76969-4.

Publisher:
Sciencia Scripts
is a trademark of
Dodo Books Indian Ocean Ltd. and OmniScriptum S.R.L publishing group

120 High Road, East Finchley, London, N2 9ED, United Kingdom
Str. Armeneasca 28/1, office 1, Chisinau MD-2012, Republic of Moldova, Europe
Managing Directors: Ieva Konstantinova, Victoria Ursu
info@omniscriptum.com

Printed at: see last page
ISBN: 978-620-8-62659-4

Summary

Thanks

I would first like to thank God for giving me the opportunity to develop this project. And for blessing me throughout my time at the Federal University of Pernambuco.

To my family for supporting me in all my endeavors and for not going out of their way to provide me with a good education. To the love of my life, Alison Rodrigues, for always having faith in me and believing in my success.

To Prof. Fàbio Campos, PH.D. for his guidance throughout this usability analysis and for believing in the project. To the teachers on the Design course at the Federal University of Pernambuco, for helping me to grow and learn more and more. To my fellow students, for making every course an adventure and always wanting to achieve the best.

To Avila Soluçôes for allowing me to use the UniClinika RIS tool, developed by the company, to design this project. To all the employees and co-workers at Avila Soluçôes for agreeing to take part and help me with my project. And to the users of the tool evaluated for answering the questionnaires that enriched this project.

Summary

With the growth of the digital market, IT (Information Technology) companies are seeing an increasing need to invest in design and usability. With competition in the market and the choice of tools available, users have become more intolerant and demanding of what they use and consume. Although usability is very important for success, it is not enough. With this new market scope, the combination of design and usability is indispensable for the product to succeed in the consumer market. Medical software goes beyond scheduling and registering patients; many help clinics from reception to collecting accounts payable and receivable. The trend is for more and more solutions to emerge for the management of clinics and hospitals. In order to improve the usability of the system so that the user is more satisfied with the software, the UniClinika RIS desktop tool will be evaluated. Following the usability principles of Jordan and Leventhal and Barnes, together with Nielsen's heuristics, the tool was evaluated and significant changes were suggested to improve it.

Keywords: usability, usability testing, heuristics, usability principles, UniClinika RIS

1. introduction:

Over the years, cell phones and computers have become indispensable tools in people's personal and business lives. The frequent use of these tools has led to the emergence of a new market, that of digital artifacts.

With the growth of the digital market, IT (Information Technology) companies are seeing an increasing need to invest in design and usability. With the competitiveness of the market and the choice of tools available, users have become more intolerant and demanding of what they use and consume.

(FALCÂO, Christianne Soares; Usability of Consumer Products: an analysis of concepts, methods and applications - 2013. 4 p.)

Considering consumer products, as explained by Jordan (2000), the usability movement has gone from 'satisfactory' to 'unsatisfactory'. In the past, users would tolerate poor usability for new functions and performances, and were surprised if a product was usable (satisfactory). Now they take it for granted that a product can be used and are unpleasantly surprised if they find it difficult to use (unsatisfactory).

Although usability is very important for success, it is not enough. With this new market environment, the combination of design and usability is indispensable for the product to succeed in the consumer market.

(FALCÂO, Christianne Soares; Usability of Consumer Products: an analysis of concepts, methods and applications - 2013. 5 p.)

In this direction, although usability is considered an important attribute for the success of products and interfaces (Jordan, 1988; Han et al., 2001; Tullis and Albert, 2008), it is clear that it alone is not enough to optimize the user-product relationship. Faced with this realization, the design community began to expand its horizon beyond usability, exploring notions such as pleasure (Jordan, 2000; Green & Jordan, 2002) and perception/emotion (Seva et al., 2011). The basis of this thinking seems to have come from the notion that a usable product is not a guarantee that people will buy it. Overbeeke et al. (2002), describes that users can often choose to use a product despite the difficulty of using it because it is challenging, seductive, fun, surprising, memorable or rewarding, resulting in the pleasure of the experience.

New desktop tools and mobile applications are reaching various areas of knowledge with the aim of facilitating the task performed by the user and even changing the way this activity is carried out. The relationship between technology and health ranges from exam machines and surgeries to assisting with simpler tasks, such as scheduling an exam via desktop and mobile devices. Despite the growing number of digital tools available to help clinics and hospitals, many still opt for the traditional paper diary.

Medical software goes beyond scheduling and registering patients; many help clinics from reception to collecting accounts payable and receivable. In order to understand the relationship between healthcare professionals and technology, an online survey *(Appendix C - Online Questionnaire Template)*, using the "Google Forms" tool, was carried out to find out which means these professionals use to schedule appointments and register their patients. The questionnaire was launched in April 2016 and lasted a month. Thirty-three health professionals responded, 87.5% of whom were doctors.

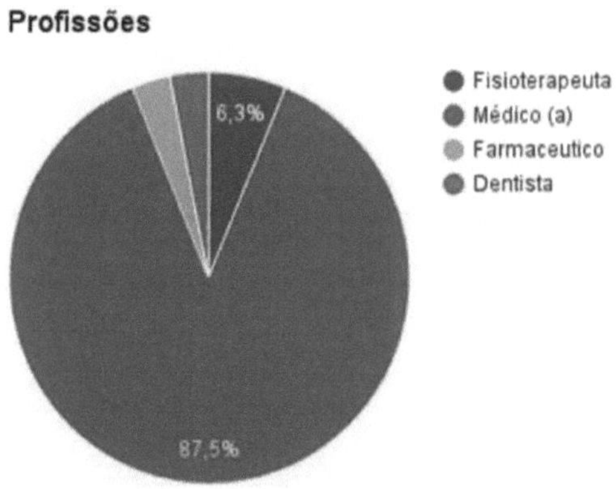

Graph 01 - Professions of the Health Professionals who answered the online questionnaire

This survey showed that paper diaries are still widely used in the health sector. Among those who answered the questionnaire, 37.5% said that they use paper diaries in their workplace. However, 34.4% said they used desktop systems, followed by 25% of diary organizing websites, which shows that they are gradually embracing digital tools.

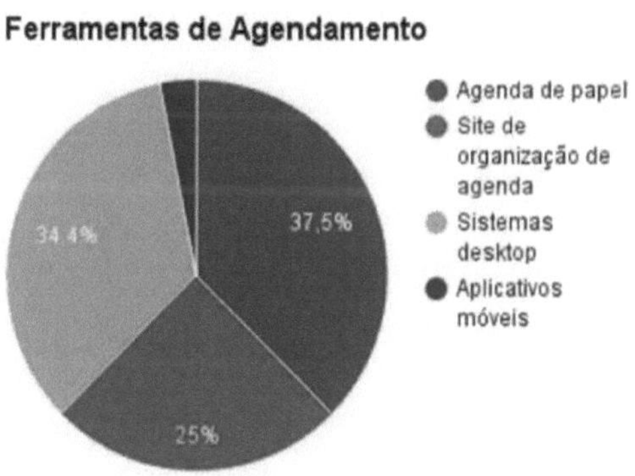

Graph 02 - Tools used by healthcare professionals to schedule and register patients

Among the list of desktop systems mentioned in the survey, it was possible to observe that some of the software used is not specialized in the health sector, but is a general business management system. But there are some that specialize in the health sector, such as Dentalist and Medsystem.

The trend is for more and more solutions to emerge for the management of clinics and hospitals. It was with this new market ambit in mind that Avila Soluçôes saw the need to create an imaging clinic management product that would meet all the clinic's needs, and UniClinika RIS was born. In order to improve the usability of the system so that the user is more satisfied with the software, the UniClinika RIS desktop tool will be evaluated according to three usability principles which will have their results compared with each other. A user survey will also be part of the analysis. And at the end, problems found in the tool, according to the usability analysis and user survey, will be listed so that they can be solved.

1.1. Problem:

Does the Service Module of the UniClinika desktop tool follow the principles of good usability? How can its usability be improved?

1.2. Objective:

1.2.1. General Objective:

This work aims to use usability principles to evaluate the Customer Service Module of the UniClinika RIS desktop tool and, based on the results, suggest improvements.

1.2.2. Specific Objective:

- Get to know the tool and its functionalities;
- Understand the flow of the task of scheduling exams and appointments;
- Taking part in training sessions offered by Avila Soluçôes to users in order to explain the tool's functionalities, observing users' main doubts and difficulties;
- Apply online and face-to-face questionnaires to find out what users think of the tool;
- Evaluate the tool according to the principles of Jordan (1998), Leventhal and Barnes and Nielsen's 10 Heuristics;
- Tool usability results and main problems;
- Suggest improvements.

1.3. Justification:

UniClinika has been in operation for over 10 years. On the market, it is the product that offers the most complete management for diagnostic imaging clinics, as it covers all their areas. Despite this, there was no designer or usability specialist in the creation process. The software has a brand and visual identity, created in 2015 to present and publicize the tool, but it doesn't follow the brand's standards, with a standard interface and no identity of its own. As a way of evaluating the tool from the point of view of a designer and usability specialist, this evaluation was set up to identify problems that were imperceptible to the developers and improvements for the user.

2. Methodological Procedures:

2.1. Research typology and structure

The work described here can be characterized as a descriptive study. According to Best apud Marconi and Lakatos (2006), descriptive research outlines the phenomenon being studied by addressing four aspects: description, recording, analysis and interpretation of current phenomena, with the aim of making it work. According to Santos et al (2011), descriptive studies are mainly related to "what" questions. Evaluative studies in the field of ergonomics, in general, can be considered descriptive research.

The work was carried out in the following stages:

• Description of the Service Module of the UniClinika RIS tool, the most recent version implemented a year ago. Regarding the functions of the module, the functions of registering new patients, registering a new requesting doctor and scheduling an examination were chosen for analysis, as they are the main functions used by the user;

• Usability analysis of the tool according to the principles of Patrick Jordan (1998), Leventhal and Barnes (2008) and Nielsen's Heuristic Evaluation (1993);

• Participation in training sessions offered by the company Avila Soluções, creator of the tool, to clients with the aim of observing the relationship between users and the tool, their main doubts and complaints. At the end, a questionnaire was administered:

• Mixed questionnaire for users after training with the following structure:

1. User profile (age, gender, experience with the product,...).

2. Information on use - opinions on possible difficulties in handling and understanding, identification of commands, and questions relating to user satisfaction with the SUS - System Usability Scale by John Brooke (1986). The SUS measures user opinions through 10 closed questions and one open question, and uses a "Likert" scale - 1 strongly disagree, 2 disagree, 3 neutral, 4 agree and 5 strongly agree. It generates an overall result on a scale of 0 to 100. The 10 questions assess:

1ª) Frequency of use of the system;

2ª) Complexity of the system;

3a) Ease of use;

4a) Assistance in using the system;

5a) Integrated system functions;

6a) System inconsistency;

7a) Fast learning;

8a) The system is cumbersome and complicated to use;

9a) Security and confidence in using the system;

10a) Learning other information to use the system

- Description and analysis of the task by the inexperienced user and application of the performance measurement test, with the following as the direct observation script: 1) performance of the tasks pre-determined by the evaluator (register new patient, register new requesting doctor and schedule exam); 2) recording of the time taken for the operations and 3) application of the questionnaire.
- A mixed questionnaire was administered to new users with the following structure:

1. User profile (age, gender, experience with the product,...).
2. Questions relating to satisfaction with use by the SUS - System Usability Scale by John Brooke (1986).

- Finalizing with suggestions for improvements to the product, with a view to facilitating its usability.

2.2. Research environment and subjects

The training environment was the José Rocha de Sà Institute, a client of Avila Soluçôes, located in Derby. With users from the clinic's Call Center area who use the UniClinika tool on a daily basis. Details of the clinic:

José Rocha de Sa Institute - Derby;

Specialty: Diagnostic imaging clinic;

Activities: Diagnostic imaging examinations;

Used by: 5 call center employees and 5 receptionists

Sample: 4 call center employees

The task analysis by the inexperienced user and the application of the performance measurement test were carried out at Avila Soluçôes with company employees who were not used to using the UniClinika tool. Company details:

Avila Soluçôes - Tamarineira;

Specialty: Information Technology (IT);

Activities: Technological solutions using Microsoft tools;

Employees: 5 directors, 2 administrative and financial staff and 25 technology staff

Tool support by: 3 employees Sample: 11 employees

2.3. Concepts:

2.1.1. Usability

The quality of an interface can be measured to assess whether it is appropriate for the user or the task for which it was developed. *Usability* is defined by ISO 9241-11 as: "*Usability is the extent to which a product can be used by certain users to achieve specific goals effectively, efficiently and satisfactorily in a certain context of use.*".

According to the book by Itiro Iida (2005), *usability* means ease and convenience in the use of products, both in the domestic and professional environments. Itiro describes good usability as "user-friendly" products and artifacts. Products should be easy to handle, intuitive and not prone to errors, generating greater user satisfaction.

2.1.2. Jordan's usability principles:

The study of usability arose from the need to create products that best suited the needs and limitations of users. With this new need arising, Jordan (1998) lists principles for good usability as guides, as well as physical characteristics, where the dimensions, weight, height and shape of the product must always respect the physical characteristics of the user, and cognitive characteristics, which refer to the knowledge that the user already has about the task they will perform with the product. The list suggested by Jordan is made up of 6 principles in which he states that the product must meet all of them in order to have good usability:

<u>1st - Evidence:</u>

The product's formal solution must clearly indicate its function and mode of operation. For example, the glass door of a public building must clearly indicate whether it must be pushed or pulled open. A metal plate with no handle can indicate that it must be pushed and, on the other side, a bar that can be grasped indicates that it must be pulled. In computing, the drawings of icons that represent functions must have clear meanings. Evidence reduces learning time and facilitates memorization, as well as reducing operating errors.

<u>2° - Consistency:</u>

Similar operations should be carried out in a similar way. This allows the user to make a positive transfer of experience previously acquired in other similar tasks. For example, people are used to opening their house and car doors. When they come across a new product that has a door, they will probably try to open it in the same way. A similar thing happens with the use of *menus* on computers.

<u>3° - Capacity:</u>

The user has certain capacities for each function, which must be respected. These capacities must not be exceeded. To drive a car, for example, both hands are occupied with the steering wheel. The other functions, such as acceleration, clutch and brake, are then transferred to the feet. The same happens with the sense organs. When vision is saturated, additional information can be transferred to other channels, such as hearing and touch. This ability is also related to the strength, precision, speed and reach required in muscular movements.

4th - Compatibility:

Meeting user expectations improves compatibility. These expectations depend on physiological and cultural factors and previous experiences. They are also related to popular stereotypes. For example, the movement of a rotary control to the right is associated with "opening" or "increasing". In many cultures, the color red is associated with danger or prohibition, as opposed to green, which signifies safety or the release of a procedure, as is the case with road signs.

5 - Preventing and correcting errors:

The products must prevent incorrect procedures. If they do occur, they must allow for quick and easy correction. In a car, starting the engine could be conditional on first putting on the seat belt and closing all the doors. When typing, some controls are often activated unintentionally. If this happens, their effect could be null or another command could be available to correct or return to the stage prior to the error.

6th - Feedback:

Products should give users feedback on the results of their action. This can be a simple "beep" indicating that a command has been triggered. In telephone calls, there is a typical noise to indicate that the call has been completed and another to indicate that the line is busy. Feedback is important so that the operator can scale his action. In many cases, they have to correct their trajectory until they reach the desired goal. The lack of this feedback can result in a lot of wastage, as in the case of the driver who drove for two hours to the next village, only to discover that he was on the wrong road. It is therefore important that this feedback takes place as quickly as possible, using signs that have the correct meaning.

2.1.3. Heumatic evaluation

Heuristic evaluation is a form of evaluation with the aim of reviewing or making decisions for a project. The evaluation follows the principles of usability, comparing the designed interface to what is expected of it, according to the principles of good usability. For Nielsen (1993), this principle aims to evaluate the usability of the proposed system with a set of evaluators who have no affinity with the system being evaluated in order to test it. Nielsen suggests 10 heuristic evaluations:

- Simplicity and natural dialog: Information should be presented logically, clearly, naturally and objectively.

- Correspondence between the language of the system and that of the user: The information contained in the system must present a clear and familiar dialog, without containing technical jargon;

- Minimize the user's memory load: The interface must be coherent and present a unified language so that the user's memory load is minimized;

• Consistency: The data must be consistent and standardized, thus preventing the user from misinterpreting it. To make it easier for users to recognize the system, the available options must have the same formatting.

• Feedback: The system needs to provide immediate feedback on the actions taken, keeping the user informed about the system;

• Clearly identified exits: The system must provide several ways out of any possible problem that may occur, i.e. the options to undo or redo a certain action must be made possible;

• Shortcuts: System shortcuts are used to optimize and speed up the process of reusing the system, so experienced users using this tool increase the speed of interaction with the system.

• Error message: Error messages should be expressed clearly and objectively, indicating precisely what the problem is and providing a constructive solution to it.

• Error prevention: When designing the system, attention must be paid to preventing possible errors that may occur during the performance of certain tasks.

• Help and documentation: The system must provide help to the user when necessary, with clear and precise information, focusing on the tasks of the user in question.

2.1.4. Leventhal and Barnes principle

After analyzing the usability models of Brian Shackel (Shackel 1986), Jakob Nielsen (Nielsen - 1993) and Kenneth Eason (Eason - 1984), Leventhal and Barnes integrated the elements of the three models to create their own.

They propose a hybrid usability model applied to systems. The model aims to determine the most important points of the three models on which they were based, in order to create a new model based on variables for evaluating good system usability. The variables are: situational variable and user interface variable.

Situational variable - task

a. Frequency: Tasks that are performed frequently are likely to include sequences already learned by the user; the specifics of the sequences may vary.

b. Rigidity: The number of paths (choices) taken through the task. The number of options that are available through the paths taken in the task.

c. Situation constraints: Situation constraint variables represent task variables that can be critical to the success or failure of an interface.

Situational variable - user

a. Expertise

i. Experienced users

ii. New users

iii. Occasional users

b. Motivation: Highly motivated users may be more likely to complete a task, even if the interface is difficult.

Interface features

a. Ease of learning: How easy the interface is for new users to learn.

b. Ease of use: How easy the interface is to operate.

c. Ease of re-learning: How easy the interface is to use once it has been learned.

d. Task suitability: A well-suited task can help the experienced or novice user map their understanding of the interface to the actual task.

e. Flexibility: Refers to the interface's ability to support new or unexpected changes in the task. E.g. supermarket cashier.

f. User satisfaction: This is the user's response to an assessment of the discrepancy between perceived expectations (or some other performance standard) and the actual performance of a product or system as perceived after use.

3. Case Study - UniClinika RIS:

The first step in a usability analysis is to get to know the product being evaluated. So I started my analysis by understanding how the UniClinika RIS product works.

UniClinika is a management tool for diagnostic imaging clinics. It was created about 10 years ago by the IT (Information Technology) company Avila Soluções. With two consolidated clients, the tool has seven modules (Scheduling, UniFinance, Billing, Inventory, UniUser, Manager and Collections) that work in specific areas of the clinic, from patient scheduling to accounts payable and receivable management.

Each module operates in a different area of the clinic and is therefore operated by different users. It is the most complete product on the market because it covers all areas of the clinic, providing software tailored to the current reality of the institution.

Understanding the UniClinika modules as a single system, where they are interconnected and dependent on each other, we can place the service module as the first stage of the system. Responsible for scheduling patients, the service module can schedule according to the times available for doctors or a slot, scheduling outside the times available in the system. The doctor performs the consultation and generates a report which is stored in the system. The exams carried out that day are accumulated, separated into batches, checked and sent to the next module, with the clinic's Conference area checking the batches. The billing module receives the batches, calculates the procedures (the entire table of values and costs is shown by the system, to speed up and facilitate the calculation) and generates the invoice. After generating the invoices, the charges are generated and sent to the next module. The billing module receives the charges and manages their disallowance status (when the plan doesn't pay for all or part of the exam) - partial disallowance, total disallowance. The financial module mirrors the collections module, but for accounts payable and receivable. The financial part manages accounts payable, partially paid and unpaid, as well as accounts receivable.

The stock module is responsible for registering and managing everything that comes in and out of the clinic. When the clinic places an order for medicines, the stock is used. When the requested medicines arrive, they are registered in the system and every time they are withdrawn, they are also registered in the system.

The manager and UniUser modules are support modules. The people in charge of the clinics have access to them and can register the doctors' schedules, change the filter of the modules to suit the clinic's needs.

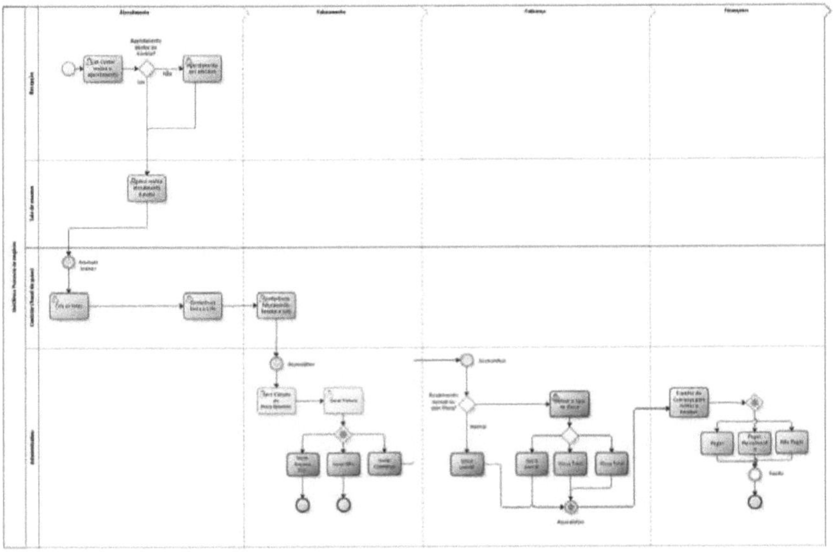

Figure 01 - Flowchart of the interaction between the UniClinika RIS modules

Features:

- Scheduling (Call Center)
- Service (reception)
- Doctor Control
- Digital report (audio recording and digital signature)
- Billing
- Electronic Billing (TISS)
- SUS Electronic Billing (BPA)
- Disallowance Management
- Finance
- Materials Control
- Shopping
- Stock
- Business Intelligence (Decision Support System)
- Automatic Exam Authorization
- Automatic preparation suggestions

- DMED
- CIHA
- Document Digitization
- Integration with SMS sending

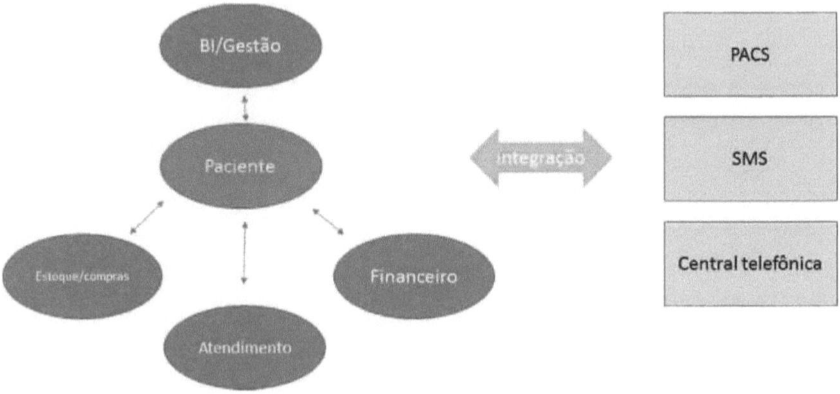

Figure 02 - UniClinika RIS system

3.1. Service Module:

The customer service module is the first module used in the UniClinika RIS system and the one chosen for the usability analysis. A year ago, a new version of this module was rolled out to customers and the evaluation will use this update. It's a module with a lot of functionalities that generate questions for users. It is used by reception and call center staff at clinics. Its main functions are to register patients, register the requesting doctor, the professional who asked the patient for the exam, and schedule exams. The tool aims to expand to the mobile universe, facilitating patient scheduling. It will allow patients to schedule exams without having to call the clinic. It is still in the development phase.

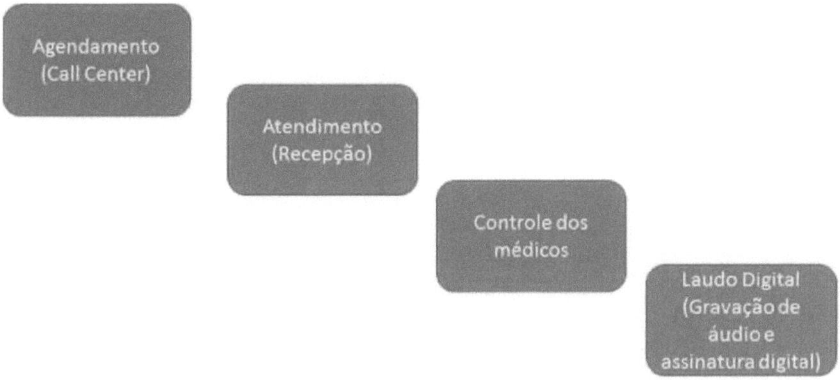

Figure 03 - Service module functionalities

Features:

- Complete agenda management with several specific filters;
- Reservation for pre-bookings;
- Confirmation of appointments by SMS;
- Customized processes by type of query;
- Agenda by type of agreement;
- It details the average ticket that each doctor can produce by scheduling according to approximate productivity;
- Quick patient registration (facilitating scheduling and pre-registration);
- Queue management;
- Service time;
- Test results;
- Updating the register;
- Patient referral flow;
- Pre-authorization of exams;
- Customized questionnaire templates for specific exams;
- Productivity control;
- Patient history;
- Customization of templates for reports, routines and prescriptions;
- Quick view of the service queue;

- Audio recording in the report;
- Digital signatures;

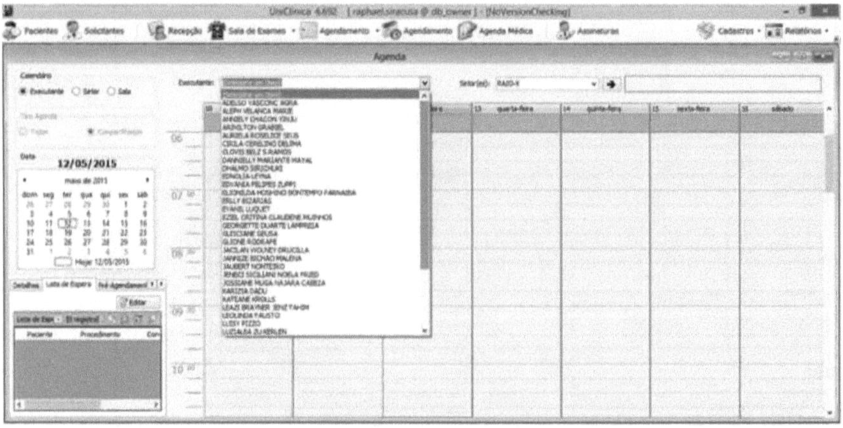

Figure 04 - Service module screen, calendar view.

3.1.1 Task analysis:

The second stage of the usability analysis was to understand the tasks performed by daily users of the service module. This module has a huge variety of functionalities that were listed earlier, but for this analysis I decided to focus on the most frequent tasks that users perform (patient registration, requester registration and exam scheduling).

Care Module - Register the patient

Objective: To register new patients for future examinations.

Steps or actions to carry it out: Open the service module and click on "Patients". The user will be redirected to the patient filter screen and on the top left-hand side there is a "New" icon, which the user will click on and be redirected to the patient registration form. The form contains Name/GD (with issuing body)/Type of ID (own, mother, parent or guardian)/CPF/Responsible (optional)/Gender/Weight/Height/Date of birth/Age (automatically filled in when the date of birth is entered)/E- mail/State/Profession/Color/Incomplete registration/CEP/Logradora (automatically filled in when the zip code is entered)/Number/Department/Borough/City/UF /Code IBGE City/Observations/Alert/Convênio (select the covenant, holder, plan, enrollment, validity)/Phone (phone, type, notes).

User: Secretaries, receptionists in hospitals and diagnostic imaging clinics.

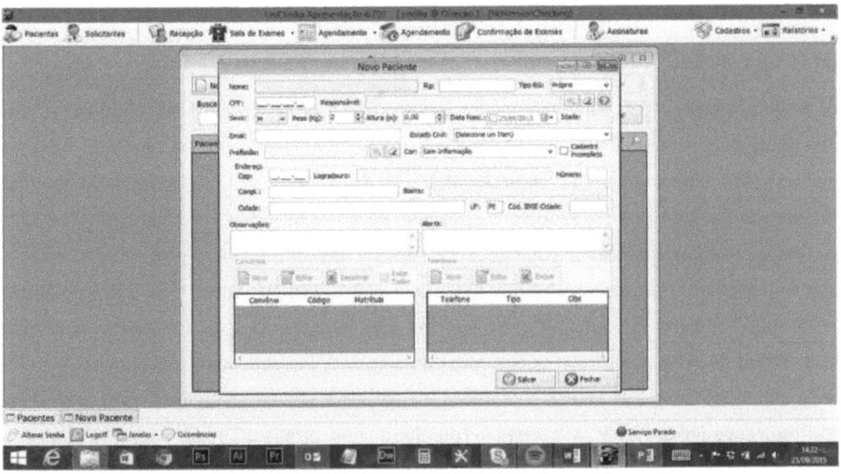

Figure 05 - Care module screen, registering a new patient.

Service Module - Register Requestor

Objective: To register a new test applicant.

Steps or actions to carry it out: Open the service module and click on "Requester". The user will be redirected to the patient filter screen and at the top left there is a "New" icon, the user will click on it and be redirected to the patient registration form. The form contains: Name/Name Report/Sex/Title/Council/No.

Cons/UF/Nascimento/CPF/Ativo/Tit/End/CEP/Logradoura/N°/Complemento/Bairro/Cidade/ UF/CNES/Executante 2/CBO/E-mail/Especialidades/Telefone.

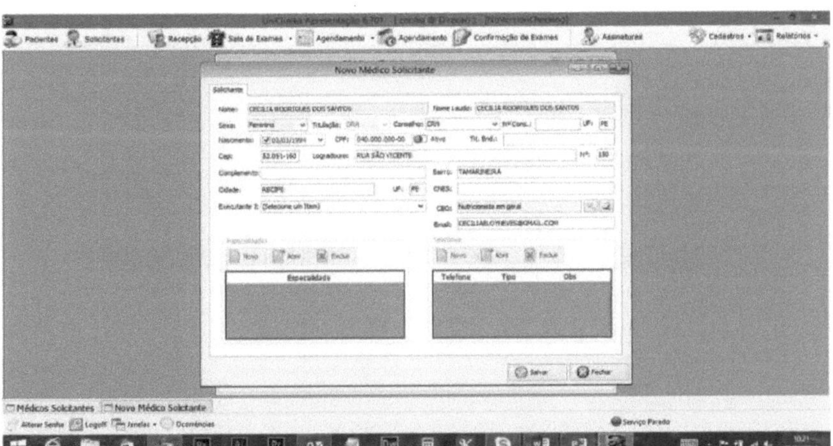

Figure 06 - Service module screen, new applicant registration view.

Service Module - Schedule Exam

Objective: To schedule exams.

Steps or actions to carry it out: Open the service module and click on "Reception". The user will be redirected to the patient filter screen and at the top left there is a "New" icon, the user will click and be redirected to the patient registration form. Another way would be to click on "Scheduling", the first one with the calendar icon, select the doctor's schedule, sector or by room. The calendar will appear with the week's or day's vacancies, if you choose to view by day, and with a double click the patient filter page will appear. Once the patient has been selected, the appointment form will open to be filled in. Through the other "Scheduling" icon, the one with the calendar icon and a clock, it is also possible to schedule. The performing doctor must be selected, the schedules will appear and it is possible to select the schedule and click on "New". The select patient screen will open and when selected, the scheduling form will open. The form has: Patient/Time/Covenant/Procedure (Procedure/Detail/Questionnaire/Done/Detail/Solicitor/No. Guide/Validity/Executor/All/Solicitation/Emission/Grade of participation/Location/No. Authorization/Val. Aut./CID(s)/Type of Authorization/Authorized/Urgency/Inpatient/Apply to all scheduled exams or exams on the form/Waiting list/Use pre-authorization/Observations)/Additional Data ()/Authorized Services ()

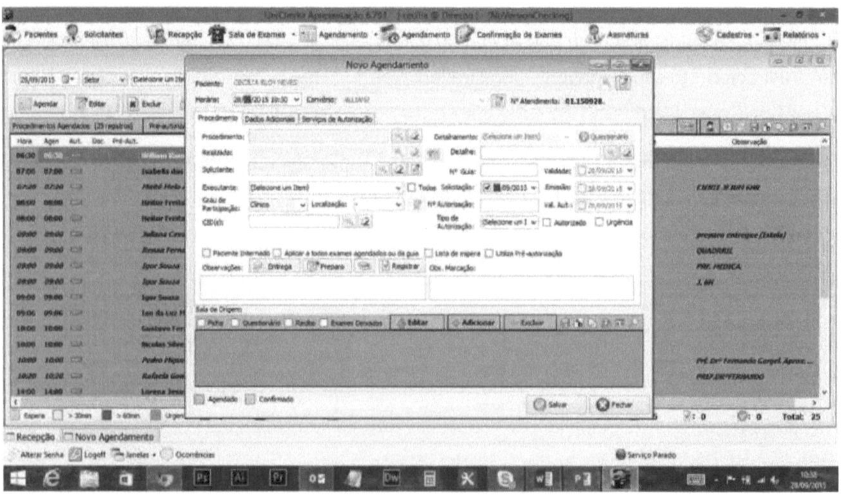

Figure 07 - Service module screen, view of the new appointment screen.

4. Usability testing and analysis

4.1. Usability pre-diagnosis

For the usability analysis of the UniClinika service module, the principles of Patrick Jordan (1998), Leventhal and Barnes (2008) and Nielsen's Heuristic Evaluation (1993) were used.

For the pre-diagnosis, the components of each screen of the module, their functions and actions of use were observed (pictograms and texts used in the commands, colors, display, shape of the control, sound information and the tasks performed). Analysis carried out by the evaluator before the results of the questionnaires and task analysis.

4.1.1. Pre-diagnosis according to Jordan's principles (1998)

Analysis presented in table form, with the evaluator's observations. The table shows three evaluation indications, red for when it doesn't meet the principles, orange for when it partially meets the principles and green for when it meets the principles.

Evidence - UniClinika's Service Module has a very intuitive name, so it's clear that it's used to schedule exams. Although the module's icon is not a good description, as it is an image of a stethoscope. When we go to the internal icons, it's a bit confusing. For example, there are two icons with the name Scheduling, which can confuse the user. By			
Scheduling icons it is possible to schedule exams, but the quickest way is through the Reception icon.			
Consistency - Although the names of the icons sometimes don't match the main functionality, as is the case with Scheduling, the module offers several ways to carry out tasks without having to close and open another window. But the alternative paths are not clear and the user doesn't always understand them.			
Capacity - The module's users are clinic receptionists and call center employees who need to be quick when registering and scheduling. Because it's on a computer, it's at the mercy of the speed of the server at the user's place of work. And it doesn't have much information, many abbreviations and acronyms are used, but there is no explanation of them.			
Compatibility - The users of the service module generally have a mental model of the paper agenda. Where staff used to memorize doctors' availability or			

have papers scattered around the room or on their desk with this information. Easy visualization of information is essential to facilitate and speed up work. And certain visualizations are only possible, easily and quickly, in certain windows of the tool.			
Error prevention and correction - The tool is made up of scheduling rules that don't allow, for example, more than one appointment to be made at the same time, and even fewer appointments to be made outside the doctors' available hours. Nor does it allow users to schedule a patient or requester who is already in the system.			
Feedback - The tool's feedback does not exist, in some functionalities such as registering a new patient, the window simply closes after the registration has been carried out, without giving any feedback to the user that the task has been carried out successfully.			

Table 01 - Pre-diagnosis according to Jordan's principles (1998)

4.1.2. Pre-diagnosis according to the concepts of Leventhal and Barnes (2008)

Analysis presented in table form, with the evaluator's observations.

Frequency: In the customer service module, we have a good separation of tasks, similar tasks are close together and you don't always have to open another screen to do another task.			
Rigidity: Taking the user's needs into account, the module provides the necessary paths without too much complexity.			
Limitations of the situation: Because it's on a computer, it's at the mercy of the server speed of the users' workplaces. And it doesn't have much information, many abbreviations and acronyms are used, but there is no explanation.			
Expertise: The program follows the structure of other desktop programs. It also follows medical terms. But some terms are not clear when it comes to identifying the task that will be performed on each screen.			
Motivation: The user has to use the program to work and they understand that it will make their work easier.			

Easy to learn: Although the tasks don't have a complex step-by-step approach, users have to get used to the medical terms and understand the acronyms and abbreviations. And understand how the tool works, which is why the company that created it offers training for users to learn how to use the system.			
Ease of use: The interface is compromised by abbreviations, acronyms, the lack of explanation, the lack of conversation from menu terms to window terms and some terms used are unclear. And some are repeated.			
Easy to re-learn: Avila Soluções offers training and, once learned, users are able to perform the tasks.			
Suitability for the task: The program has a good division, where it is easy to locate and learn the path of the task. It's just the nomenclature that can be confusing at first.			
Flexibility: The program always leaves the top menu visible, regardless of which window you open. The icon to close the window is always visible, as well as some tabs at the bottom that show the windows that are open so that the user can access them without any problems.			
User satisfaction: The program offers all the resources for the user to carry out all their tasks more easily, but it is not intuitive and does not offer all the visualizations easily to the user (visualization of doctors' schedules, for example).			

Table 02 - Pre-diagnosis according to the Leventhal and Barnes model (2008)

4.1.3. Pre-diagnosis according to Nielsen's heuristic evaluation (1993)

Analysis presented in table form, with the evaluator's observations.

Simple and natural dialog - The route to complete the tasks is simple and several ways are offered to complete the same task, but the information is not clear and there is a pollution of elements that are often not necessary.			
Speak the user's language - The icons and terms used are common, with some medical terms, but that's not a problem for the user. But they're not clear and there's no explanation of each term, which ends up generating doubt.			

Minimize the user's memory load - Information is not clear, users still have to memorize some information to speed up the process, due to the lack of time to view, for example, a doctor's schedule at the time of the appointment.			
scheduling.			
Consistency - Although the names of the icons sometimes don't match the main functionality, as is the case with Schedules, the module offers several ways to carry out tasks without having to close and open another window. But the alternative paths are not clear and the user doesn't always understand them.			
Feedback - There is no clear feedback, the user finishes the task without knowing if it was successful or not.			
Clearly marked exits - No matter which screen is accessed, the top menu is always in view and a bottom bar with the open screens is also shown. On all screens it is possible to "Cancel" and "Close" the action without difficulty, as well as to switch screens easily and intuitively.			
Shortcuts - Although some icons can be confusing, all areas of the tool are easy to access, as there are icons for all of them.			
Good error messages - Although the registration form doesn't show which information must be filled in, the error messages are straightforward, always showing what needs to be filled in for the activity to be carried out.			
Error prevention - It offers easy and intuitive routes to all the screens and functionalities, but fails to provide users with instructions. And due to the lack of feedback, the user is left in doubt as to whether the task was successful or not.			
Help and documentation - There is no help icon or instructions on the screens on how to perform the tasks.			

Table 03 - Pre-diagnosis according to Nielsen's 10 heuristics (1993)

4.2. Questionnaire results

4.2.1. Questionnaire with daily users

The questionnaire *(Appendix A - Model of Questionnaire applied after Training)* was carried out after training mediated by an employee of the Avila Soluções company. The data collected is presented in tabular form to facilitate visualization. Three daily users of the customer service module answered the questionnaire.

4.2.1.1. Personal Data

Questions	User 1	User 2	User 3
Age	20-30 years	41-50 years	31-40 years
Sex	Female	Female	Female
Do you have any	No	No	No
disability/limitation?			
Profession	Call Center	Call Center	Call Center
Education	Higher Education Incomplete	Higher education completed	Elementary school incomplete
Have you used any other appointment scheduling tool before?	No	No	No

Table 04 - Training record - User's personal information

4.2.1.2. Information on using UniClinika RIS - Service Module

Questions	User 1	User 2	User 3
How important was the training for you?	Important	Important	Essential for carrying out the task
Do you find the layout and layout information easy to understand?	Neutral	Neutral	Neutral
Regarding the information (pictographic and/or textual) displayed on the Service Module layout, do you find it easy to understand?	Neutral	I disagree	I agree
What kind of problems do you identify in this information?	Amount of information	Amount of information	Readability
Regarding the feedback provided by the Service Module during the activation of the program's functions, do you consider it adequate?	Neutral	I disagree	Neutral

Table 05 - Training record - Information on using the tool

4.2.1.3. SUS Table (System Usability Scale)

	Strongly disagree	I disagree	Neutral	I agree	Totally agree
1. I think I'd like to use this system often		33,33%	66,67%		
	1	2	3	4	5
2. I found the system unnecessarily complex			100%		
	1	2	3	4	5
3. I found the system easy to use	33,33%	33,33%	33,33%		
	1	2	3	4	5
4. I thought I would need the support of a technician to be able to use this system				66,67%	33,33%
	1	2	3	4	5
5. The functions of this system were well integrated	33,33%	66,67%			
	1	2	3	4	5
6. I found this system very inconsistent			66,67%	33,33%	
	1	2	3	4	5
7.I imagine that most people would learn to use this system quickly	33,33%	66,67%			
	1	2	3	4	5
8. I found this system very complicated to use			33,33%	33,33%	33,33%
	1	2	3	4	5
9. I felt very confident using this system	33,33%	66,67%			
	1	2	3	4	5
10. I would need to learn a lot of things before continuing to use this system		33,33%			66,67%
	1	2	3	4	5

Table 06 - Training record - SUS table result

The SUS (System Usability Scale) results collected with these questionnaires were an average of 28.33, well below good system usability. The result was obtained from the arithmetic mean of the results of each questionnaire, which were 32.5, 40, 12.5 points.

4.2.2. Questionnaire with new users

The questionnaire *(Appendix B - Questionnaire Model applied after the Tasks)* was carried out after the new users had completed the tasks of registering a new patient, registering a new applicant and scheduling an examination. The data collected is presented in the form of graphs to facilitate visualization, with the exception of the SUS table, which will be presented in the form of a table with percentages. Three daily users of the service module answered the questionnaire.

4.2.2.1 Personal data

1. age

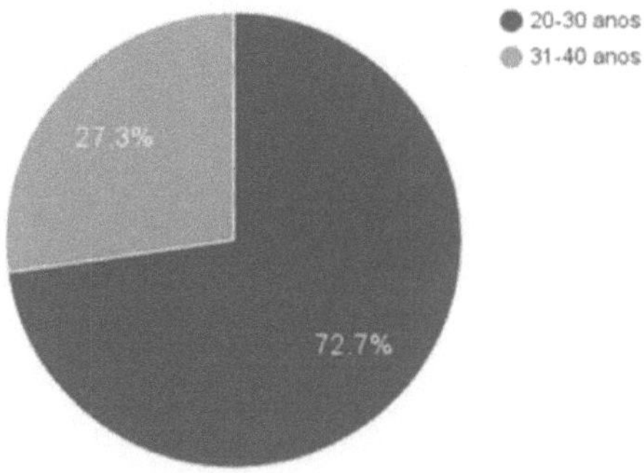

Graph 03 - Age group of new users

2. Sex

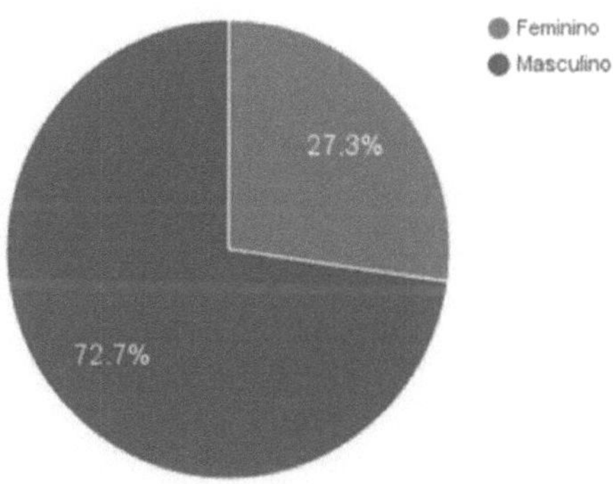

Graph 04 - Sex of novice users

4. Profession

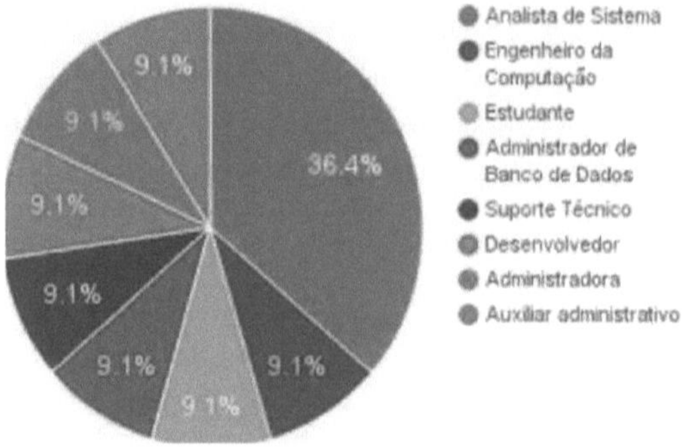

Graph 05 - Professions of new users

5. Education

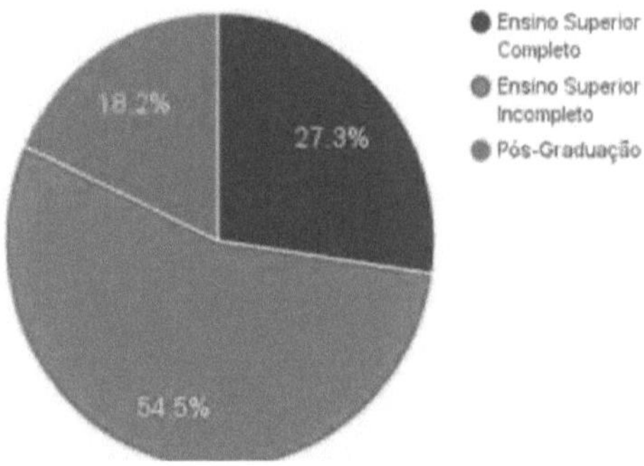

Graph 06 - Education level of new users

4.2.2.2. SUS Scale (System Usability Scale)

	Strongly disagree	I disagree	Neutral	I agree	Totally agree
1. I think I'd like to use this system often		18,18%	27,27%	54,54%	
	1	2	3	4	5
2. I found the system unnecessarily complex		45,45%	18,18%	36,36%	
	1	2	3	4	5
3. I found the system easy to use		45,45%	36,36%	18,18%	
	1	2	3	4	5
4. I thought I would need the support of a technician to be able to use this system	9,09%	27,27%	9,09%	36,36%	18,18%
	1	2	3	4	5

5. The functions of this system were well integrated			27,27%	72,72%	
	1	2	3	4	5

6. I found this system very inconsistent		72,72%	18,18%	9,09%	
	1	2	3	4	5

7.I imagine that most people would learn to use this system quickly	9,09%	36,36%	9,09%	45,45%	
	1	2	3	4	5

8. I found this system very complicated to use		63,63%	18,18%	18,18%	
	1	2	3	4	5

9. I felt very confident using this system	18,18%	18,18%	45,45%	18,18%	
	1	2	3	4	5

10. I would need to learn a lot of things before continuing to use this system	18,18%	18,18%	18,18%	36,36%	9,09%
	1	2	3	4	5

Table 07 - Results of the SUS table with new users

The results of the System Usability Scale (SUS) collected with these questionnaires were an average of 53.15 points, slightly above average. The result was obtained from the arithmetic mean of the results of each questionnaire, which were 60, 32.5, 60, 65, 42.2, 60, 42.5, 27.5, 67.5, 70, 57.5 points.

The result of this questionnaire was better, as far as the points collected by the SUS table are concerned. Taking an arithmetic average of both averages acquired during the process, we have 47.83 points. It is therefore considered a poor and unsatisfactory system for the user. Since SUS scores below 60 represent poor systems and user dissatisfaction, and scores above 80 represent very good experiences with a high level of satisfaction.

4.3. Recording and analysis of tasks

Before applying both questionnaires, records were made by observing the user's relationship with the tool being evaluated.

4.3.1. Recording and analysis - Training

The first record was made on May 5, 2016 during a training session offered by the company that created UniClinika to present the new functionalities of the Service Module to the daily users of the client Instituto José Rocha de Sà, Derby, Recife/PE.

Three employees from the clinic's call center took part in the training, as well as two employees from the support department and one from the board of directors. The training lasted about 1.5 hours.

The purpose of this visit was to present only the new features, but some of the system's errors and problems faced by users on a day-to-day basis were also raised.

It was possible to see that, although the new functionalities had already been implemented in the clinic for about a year, they were not being used. This can be explained by the fact that the new features were not applied to the existing program. They created another service module with the new features and the clinic's users didn't bother to use it because they were already used to the old one. And even after training, they weren't very excited about the new module. In the call center room, we could see several papers scattered around the room with doctors' schedules and other information used daily by the employees, who missed having this information easily visualized in the tool. Some of the functions they missed most were:

- Easy and quick viewing of the doctor's schedule, regardless of the screen they are on;
- Storing the patient's/applicant's registered information so that, even if the system crashes, everything that has been filled in will not be lost. This error will only occur if the user reserves the information filled in;
- Doctors' schedules should be easier to view and accessible from any area of the program;
- Difficulty changing appointments. It happens a lot that the patient changes dates quickly and in order to make the change the employees have to close the screen and check the calendar to see the doctor's availability;
- I've noticed that employees miss more specific filters to speed up the scheduling process;
- They didn't approve of the new agenda view because it was more general, while the old one showed more important information.

Even after training, they didn't feel confident using the tool without support during the adaptation period. In addition to the problems of the functionalities not meeting all expectations. Routine problems were also raised which cannot be said to be a problem with the tool, as they could be a problem with the clinic's local server and the machines used. For example, when the tool closes during a task, some said that it happens when they enter the exam code and click "Enter" instead of "tab", others said that it closes during scheduling.

The errors were listed and taken to Avila Soluções to be analyzed and adjusted.

4.3.2. Recording and analysis - Tasks

The second record was made at the Avila Soluções company during the evaluation of the service module, where each employee of the company, who had never used the tool before, had to carry out three activities: register a new patient with their data, register a new requester with the data pre-established by the evaluator and schedule an exam.

Ten employees took part in the analysis and the time taken to perform the tasks varied:

	1°	2°	3°	4°	5°	6°	7°	8°	9°	10°	Average
Patient Registration	16min	3min	4min	7min	2min	16min	4min	3min	3min	3min	6.1 min
Register Applicant	5min	3min	2min	4min	2min	5min	3min	3min	2min	3min	3.2 min
Schedule a test	13min	7min	6min	7min	5min	13min	7min	9min	4min	7min	7.8 min

Table 08 - Time taken by new users to complete tasks

While carrying out the tasks, it was possible to observe that all the new users had no problem finding the screen for registering the patient and requester. Although they were unfamiliar with the term "requester", there was an icon with the same term that didn't raise any questions. Some had trouble filling in the necessary information, because there is a lot of information and it doesn't show what needs to be filled in. It was also possible to analyze that when both registrations were finished, because there was no success message, everyone felt the need to check another screen to see if the registration had been successful. In both registration forms, there are spaces that the user only has access to fill in after clicking "save" once, which generated a lot of doubt when carrying out the tasks.

During the scheduling task, the paths used varied and some required the assessor's help to complete the task. Only the first user used the "reception" screen to make the appointment, which was the quickest way. The others were always directed to the "scheduling" screens, one showing the doctor's schedule in list form and the other in calendar form. Both paths generated a lot of doubt, as it is necessary to select an executing doctor, which some confused with the requesting doctor previously registered. Of the 10 people assessed, 3 needed the assessor's help to complete the task of scheduling an exam.

At the end of the questionnaire, there was a space reserved for suggestions and opinions from those evaluated about the tool. A number of responses were obtained with errors encountered during the tasks and user difficulties:

"The fields used in the search should be displayed on the screen with the results. Format editing in the height field. Marital status without content. List of professions incomplete. Agreement registration not enabled. Responsible person not required. CPF not included. Why does it only enable health insurance after patient registration? No CBO search option. Difference between CBO and specialties? Format only accepts upper case records and there are lower case records. When selecting a client in the appointment, it is necessary to enter the saved record in order to select. Detail field without content. Search screens must be entered with the smart option checked. Executor without content."

"I found it easy to use, but I would need training."

"The terms used didn't seem clear to me, especially when it came to scheduling an exam. I would never have imagined that an appointment would be made in 'reception'."

"Improve the design interface to be more intuitive."

"Interesting in terms of the objective of gathering information from the point of view of the user of a given system."

"Overall, the system meets the requirements needed to carry out the registration tasks, but the path to them is not always intuitive enough."

"Some factors are inconsistent, there are bugs in patient registration."

"There should be a more robust feedback system."

"I think the ergonomics of the system could be improved. When you press "tab" the flow doesn't follow the natural line on some screens. I also missed some masks for telephone fields. Another problem identified was an SQL error when completing an operation with an error. I tried to schedule a procedure on a date prior to today."

4.3.3. Recording and analysis - Training 2

After the training session on May 5, 2016 at the José Rocha de Sà Institute, Avila Soluçôes, based on the problems raised in the last training session, applied some of the client's requests to the tool. It added a view by day, rather than just by time of day, and applied some of the filters requested. Based on these changes, new training was offered to show the progress and encourage the use of the new Service Module.

The new training was held on July 1 at the José Rocha de Sà Institute with 3 call center employees, 1 support employee and 1 from the management team. The training started at 9am and finished at 11.40am. The new module was presented again, from the beginning, and the call center employees followed along on their machines while it was being demonstrated. When the new visualization per day was presented, they were quite satisfied, but as the demonstration went on, new problems were pointed out and requests made.

The employees said they were very satisfied with the old module and were very reluctant to switch to the new one. They argued that some of the functions they used a lot and considered indispensable for carrying out their daily tasks quickly had been removed. They existed in the old module, but no longer in the new one. This was the case with the "change" icon, which made it easy to change the doctor carrying out an appointment without having to edit the form. Just select the doctor to be changed, the new one and click on the "change" icon. The training was then paused and space opened up for the necessary needs and adjustments to be raised and listed.

In addition to the filters requested in the other training, which are yet to be implemented, other adjustments have been requested:

- Back with the "change" icon;

- When you select the existing doctors, only show the clinic, because it is a network of examination clinics and you end up showing all the doctors;
- Do not allow an exam that a doctor does not perform to be marked, there is no filter to select the exam and show only the doctors who perform it;
- Automatic saving, so that even if the program closes, which they said happens frequently, the patient's data is not lost;
- Make it easier to view patients' contact numbers;
- Some screens lack descriptive captions and color descriptions;
- Also show the display by day for sector and room schedules, as some exams are not scheduled by the doctors' schedules, but by the sector and room schedules;

After the adjustments had been listed, the board made it clear that the migration to the new agenda will only take place when all the requests have been made. The new agenda has to be used because of the smartphone app that will be launched so that patients can book without having to call.

The meeting made it clear that the changes made to the new scheduling system were not properly aligned with users. Functionalities were excluded without prior research into whether they were useful or not. Talking to the client at all stages is extremely important, as they are the only ones who know what they need in order to carry out their tasks on a day-to-day basis.

4.4. Usability diagnosis

After the results presented in the records and analyses made with daily users and new users and in the pre-diagnosis, it was possible to see that the UniClinika RIS service module has all the necessary functionalities for the day-to-day care of a diagnostic imaging clinic, but without a good layout and hierarchization of the information. It is not an intuitive tool and lacks user feedback.

In order to improve user interaction with the tool, problems with the tool that need to be solved have been listed:

- Explore the tool's branding more and apply the manual's standards to the tool. Applying the brand when opening the tool, set it as the background of the main screen, not all windows.

Figure 08 - UniClinika RIS home screen

- Change the icons of the modules to speak more to the brand and better describe the functionality of each module.

Figure 09 - Suggested icons for each module

- Don't repeat the name of the icons. Even though they have different functions and different icons, leaving them with the same name will confuse the user. Change the names to Calendar, which displays the calendar, and Schedule, which displays the schedule according to the doctors' availability.

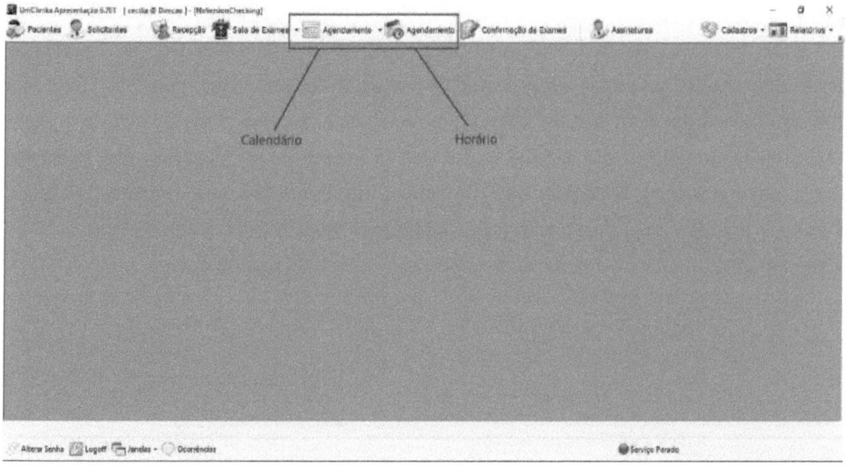

Figure 10 - Service Module screen

- In the new patient and request form, mark the information that is not required to complete the task. And adjust so that when the user uses the "tab" key, the transition to the next piece of information is linear. It is also important that when the zip code is entered, the Yogradoura information is automatically displayed, without the user having to click on a key for this information to appear. And that users have access to all areas of the form, including telephone and health insurance, which are only released after all the previous information has been filled in and the first click on "save". If it is necessary to enter the issuing body and state of the ID, it is important to make this clear with a mask or example.

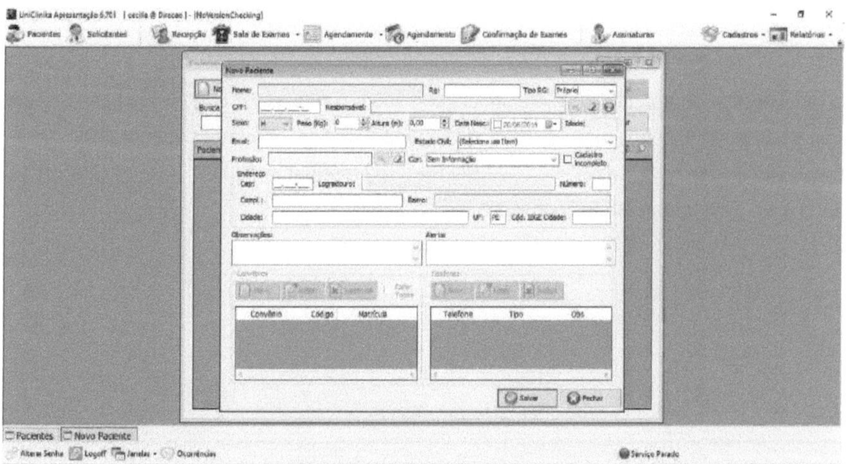

Figure 11 - Service Module screen - New patient

- It's very important that information such as "sex" doesn't come with an automatic answer, it comes without a pre-selected answer for the user to select. The "marital status" area is not working, it doesn't show an option and it doesn't even allow the user to write anything. The "Incomplete registration" checkbox is not visible and it should be located at the end of the registration form and when the user closes the form with the incomplete registration, instead of simply closing it, there should be a message telling them that the registration is incomplete and that they can select the checkbox to save and finish filling it in later. Be careful with terms like "sex" or "color", because nowadays there are more appropriate terms and options too. These are not incorrect terms, but they can cause embarrassment for some patients and be seen as a form of prejudice.

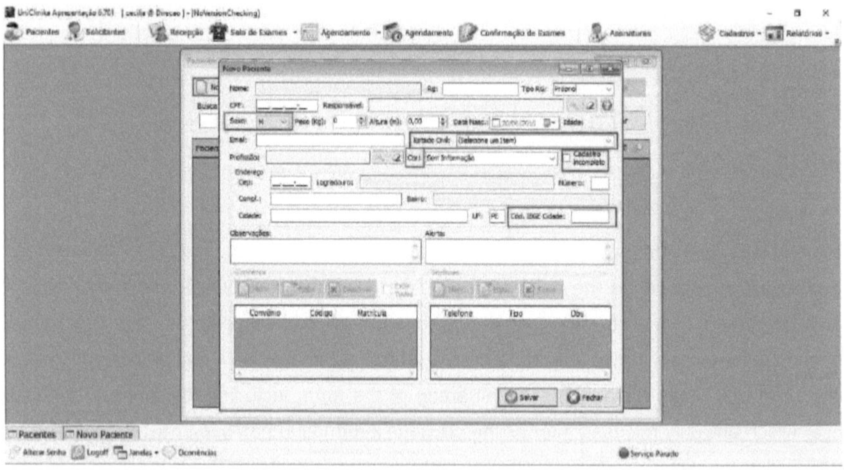

Figure 12 - Service Module screen - New Patient

- At the end of any task, whether registration or scheduling, it is important that there is a message informing the user that the activity has been successfully completed.

- In the selection of professions, there should be a more complete list of professions, many are not listed. It's important to put "housewife" and "domestic worker", they are different professions. Add an automatic search bar when you open the list of professions, without having to click on the magnifying glass icon for the tab to appear.

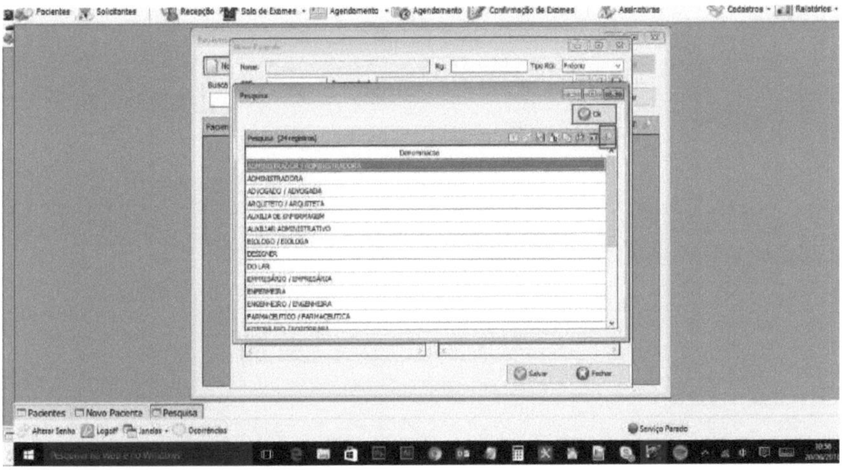

Figure 13 - Service Module Screen - List of Professions

- It's important to keep the lettering standard on all screens, whether it's all capital letters or capital and small letters.

- When one screen appears on top of another, the buttons get confused. During the analysis, some users clicked on the wrong button during the task. You could leave the background screen disabled so that this error doesn't occur.

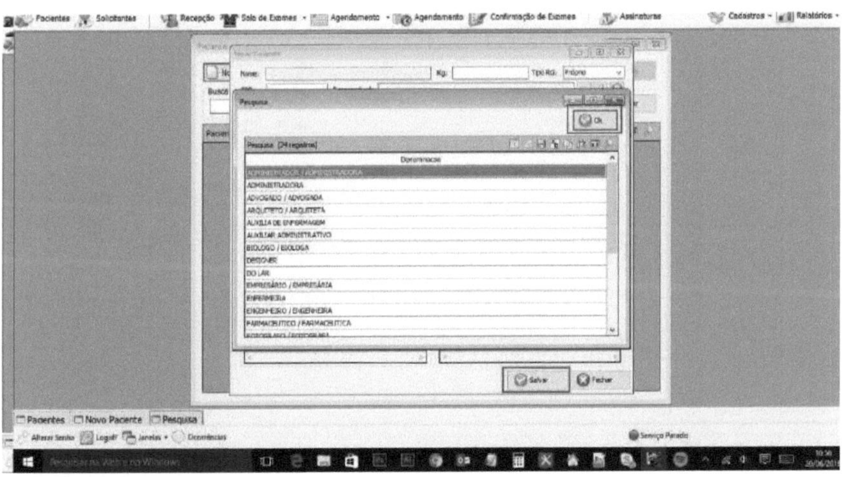

Figure 14 - Service Module screen - List of professions

- When it comes to adding a plan to the register, all plans have a standard, whether it's the number of characters or the type of characters. One way of preventing errors when registering the plan's enrollment number is to leave these rules pre-established so as to reduce the number of errors when registering.

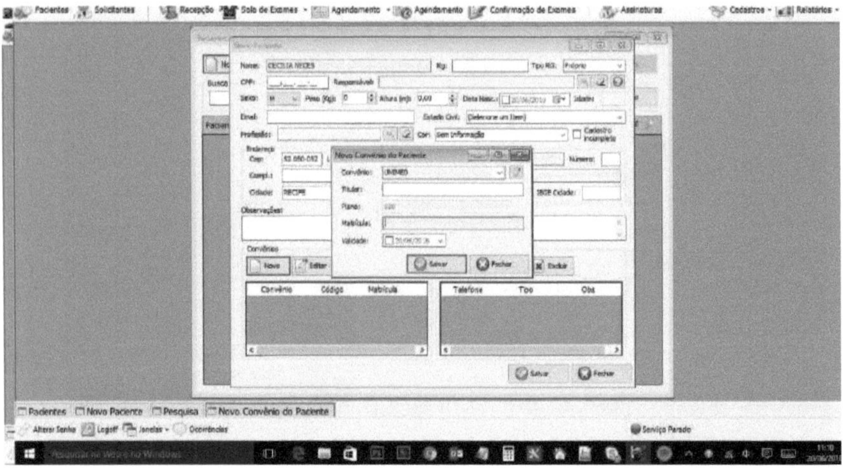

Figure 15 - Service Module screen - Add Agreement

- It's always important to have a connection between the menu option selected and the name of the window. If I click on Scheduling, the name of the window cannot be Agenda. This makes it easier for the user to learn and prevents them from selecting the wrong option or even not finding what they are looking for.

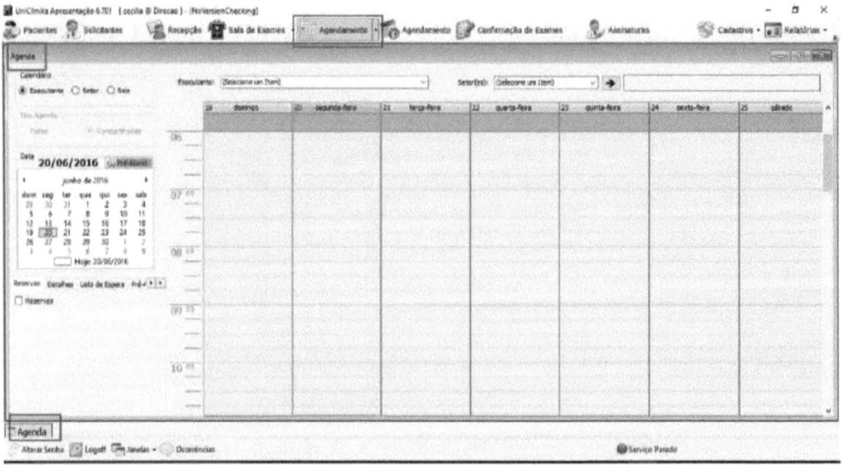

Figure 16 - Service Module screen - Calendar

- In the side tab of the calendar, there are only tabs with checkboxes that show your information when you select them. This extra click is irrelevant, there is just one more step for the user. Leave the information already selected, because there is no other information to be shown in the tabs.

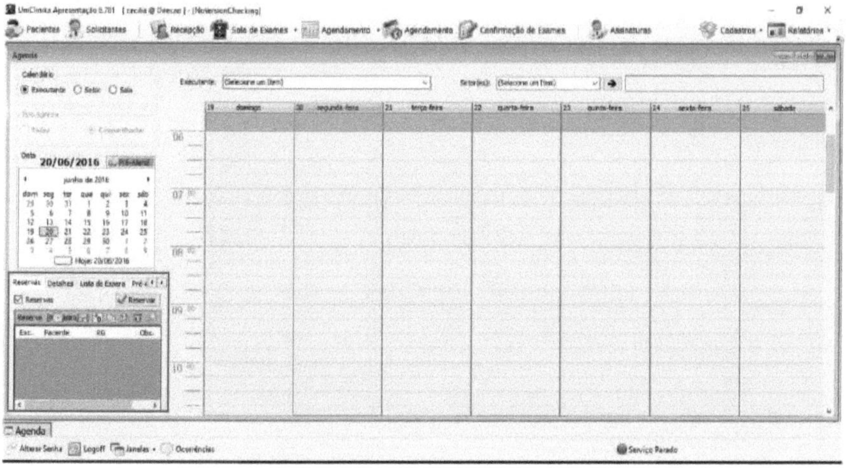

Figure 17 - Service Module screen - Calendar

- The system doesn't allow you to register an already registered doctor as a patient. A doctor can also be a patient. The system cannot allow two patients with the same information or two doctors with the same information. But a doctor can carry out an examination at the clinic, want to register as a patient and the system would not allow this action because is already registered as the requesting doctor, for example.

- Ensure that information is automatically saved to avoid rework if the system closes on its own, i.e. closed due to user error.

- Make it easier to change dates and times when making an appointment. Currently it is not recommended to change through the new appointment window, as it shows the days/times outside the doctor's availability, which would cause an error and would not allow the task to be completed. If the doctor is already selected, when showing the dates/times only show the doctor's availability. Do not show past dates and times as an option.

- Explanation of terms, acronyms, and some icons are interesting so that new users, without training, can perform all the necessary tasks without problems.

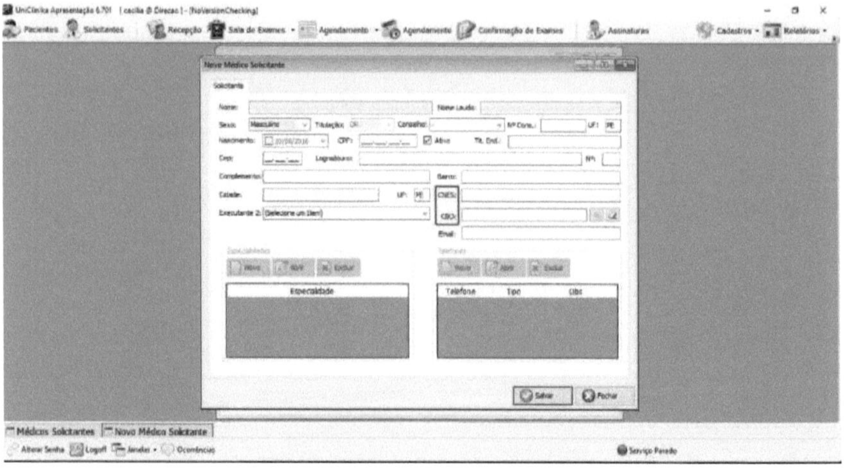

Figure 16 - Service Module screen - New Requesting Doctor

With these changes in place, users will feel more confident when using it and it will become more intuitive for new users.

5. Conclusion

The purpose of this study was to evaluate the latest version of the UniClinika RIS desktop tool, specifically the service module, according to the usability principles of Jordan (1998), the usability model of Leventhal and Barnes (2008) and the heuristics of Nielsen (1992). As a result, the analysis of the tool proved to be unsatisfactory, even though it has all the necessary functions for diagnostic imaging clinics.

During the training offered by Avila Soluções on May 5, 2016, it was possible to see how difficult it was for users to adapt to the tool's functionalities. Several doubts were raised during the training and even after the explanation, users didn't feel confident to use the tool on their own on a daily basis. Requests were made for adjustments to the tool, including new filters and more specific visualizations.

After the first training session, the client's requests were met by the company and the implementation began. On July 1st, another training session was held with the same users. Even though some requests had already been met and the others were in progress, more requests were made. They were still very reluctant to use the new module and said they would only use it once all the adjustments had been made. They argued that functionalities that were essential for day-to-day tasks had been excluded from the new module, even though they existed in the old one. This shows that there was a lack of communication with the client when the latest version was being planned.

The second record was made at Avila Soluções, during the evaluation of the service module, where each employee of the company, who had never used the tool before, had to carry out three activities: register a new patient with their details, register a new requester with the details pre-established by the evaluator and schedule an exam. The results collected showed that the tool is simple, but not intuitive and confuses the user with the lack of feedback and descriptions of the activities. The results of the data collected during the tasks showed that patient and requester registration is quite intuitive, as it has direct icons, but the mandatory information was not well signposted, nor did it have a description and the lack of feedback confused everyone at the end of the task. But when scheduling exams, there were several problems. The easiest way to schedule an exam would be through the "Reception" icon, but the existence of two "Scheduling" icons confused the user, causing many to have difficulty finishing the task.

The results of the questionnaires were unsatisfactory. The results of the questionnaires administered after the training showed how difficult it is for users to use the tool. And how dependent they are on memorizing doctors' schedules and day-to-day support. While the questionnaires applied after carrying out the tasks showed that users don't find the tool complex, but say that it isn't intuitive and that they missed the feedback and help information. The results of the SUS table applied on the day of the training showed a very low average, 28.33 points, while those of the new users showed a slightly higher average, 53.15 points. The final average was slightly lower at 47.83 points. This shows that improvements and adjustments are needed to the tool.

As a way of improving the system's performance and user satisfaction, the proposed work also suggested a series of changes. More than 10 changes were suggested, including design and usability. The analysis, records and suggested changes will be passed on to the company Avila Soluções, creator of UniClinika RIS, so that they are aware of them and can apply the adjustments.

6. Bibliographical references

FALCÂO, Christianne Soares; *Usability of Consumer Products: an analysis of concepts, methods and applications* - 2013.

FERNANDES, Walquir da Silva; *Verification of the conformity of current usability heuristics when applied to medical diagnostic imaging equipment*. 2014. Dissertation (Graduate Program in Design) - Federal University of Pernambuco, Recife.

NETO, Edvar Vilar; *A contribution to a new usability through the compilation of heuristics for devices with multimodal interaction*. 2013. Dissertation (Master's) - Federal University of Pernambuco, Recife.

ACIOLY, Angélica; TORRES, Caroline; ELOY, Cecilia; SILVA, Ester; *Usability Analysis of Remote Controls for Split Air Conditioners*. 2013. Final paper for Ergonomics and Usability - Federal University of Pernambuco, Recife.

BROOKE, John. SUS - A quick and dirty usability scale. Available at: http://www.usabilitynet.org/trump/documents /Suschapt.doc. Accessed Mar.2013

LEVENTHAL, Laura; BARNES, Julie. Usability Engineering: process, products and example. USA: Pearson Prentice Hall. 2008.

JORDAN, Patrick W. An Introduction to Usability. London: Taylor & Francis. 1998.

IIDA, ITIRO; Ergonomics: design and production / Itiro Iida - 2ª ed. ver. e ampl. - Sâo Paulo: Blucher, 2005. 320 p.

Appendix A - Training Questionnaire Template

Research Title: **Usability Analysis of the UniClinika RIS Product**

Research objective: To **analyze user interaction with the UniClinika RIS Service Module, according to usability principles.**

Group members: **Cecilia Eloy Neves.**

Tool to be evaluated: **UniClinika RIS - Service Module**

PART 1 - PERSONAL DATA

1 - Age: under 20 ( ) 20-30 ( ) 31-40 ( ) 41-50 ( ) 51-60 ( ) over 60 ( )

2 - Sex: Female ( ) Male ( )

3 - Do you have a disability/limitation? No ( ) Yes ( ), which one?

4 - Profession: ______________________________

5 - Education:

Elementary School Complete ( ) Elementary School Incomplete ( ) High School Complete ( ) High School Incomplete ( ) Higher Education Complete ( ) Higher Education Incomplete ( ) Postgraduate ( )

6 - Have you used any other appointment scheduling tool before?

No ( ) Yes ( ) Which? ______________________________

I PART 2 - INFORMATION ON USING UNICLINIKA RIS - SERVICE MODULE I

7 - How important was the training for you?

Not very important ( ) Minimally important ( ) Important ( ) Very important ( ) Essential for the task ( )

8 - Regarding the information, do you consider the layout and arrangement of the information to be EASY TO UNDERSTAND?

Strongly disagree ( ) Disagree ( ) Neutral ( ) Strongly agree ( ) Agree ( )

9 - Regarding the information (pictographic and/or textual) displayed on the Service Module layout, do you consider it to be EASY TO UNDERSTAND?

Strongly disagree ( ) Disagree ( ) Neutral ( ) Strongly agree ( ) Agree ( )

9.1 What kind of problem do you identify in this information?

Legibility ( ) Understanding its meaning ( ) Sizing ( ) Color/Contrast ( )

Quantity of information ( ) Other ( ) which? ______________________________

10 - Regarding the feedback provided by the Service Module when triggering the program's functions, do you consider it ADEQUATE?

Strongly disagree ( ) Disagree ( ) Neutral ( ) Strongly agree ( ) Agree ( )

11 - Regarding your satisfaction with using the service module, please answer the following questions: (System Usability Scale, **© Digital Equipment Corporation, 1986)**

	Strongly disagree	**I disagree**	**Neutral**	**I agree**	**Totally agree**
1. I think I'd like to use this system often	1	2	3	4	5
2. I found the system unnecessarily complex	1	2	3	4	5
3. I found the system easy to use	1	2	3	4	5
4. I thought I would need the support of a technician to be able to use this system	1	2	3	4	5
5. The functions of this system were well integrated	1	2	3	4	5
6. I found this system very inconsistent	1	2	3	4	5
7.I imagine that most people would learn to use this system quickly	1	2	3	4	5
8. I found this system very complicated to use	1	2	3	4	5
9. I felt very confident using this system	1	2	3	4	5
10. I would need to learn a lot of things before continuing to use this system	1	2	3	4	5

What are your thoughts on this tool/suggestion?

Thank you for taking part in this survey.

Appendix B - Model of the questionnaire applied after carrying out the tasks

Research Title: **Usability Analysis of the UniClinika RIS Product**

Research objective: **To analyze user interaction with the UniClinika RIS Service Module, according to usability principles.**

Group members: **Cecilia Eloy Neves.**

Tool to be evaluated: **<u>UniClinika RIS - Service Module</u>**

PART 1 - PERSONAL DATA 1 - Age: under 20 years old ( ) 20-30 years old ( ) 31-40 years old ( ) 41-50 years old ( ) 51-60 years old ( ) over 60 years old ( )

2 - Sex: Female ( ) Male ( )

3 - Do you have a disability/limitation? No ( ) Yes ( ), which one?

4 - Profession:____

5 - Schooling: Complete elementary school ( ) Elementary School Incomplete ( ) Education

High School Completed ( ) High School Incomplete ( ) Higher Education Completed ( ) Higher Education Incomplete ( ) Postgraduate ( )

I PART 2 - INFORMATION ON THE USE OF UNICLINIKA RIS - SERVICE MODULE 6 - Regarding your satisfaction with using the service module, please answer the following questions: (System Usability Scale, **© Digital Equipment Corporation, 1986)**

	Strongly disagree	I disagree	Neutral	I agree	Totally agree
1. I think I'd like to use this system often	1	2	3	4	5
2. I found the system unnecessarily complex	1	2	3	4	5
3. I found the system easy to use	1	2	3	4	5
4. I thought I would need the support of a technician to be able to use this system	1	2	3	4	5
5. The functions of this system were well integrated	1	2	3	4	5

6. I found this system very inconsistent					
	1	2	3	4	5

7.I imagine that most people would learn to use this system quickly					
	1	2	3	4	5
8. I found this system very complicated to use					
	1	2	3	4	5

9. I felt very confident using this system					
	1	2	3	4	5

10. I would need to learn a lot of things before continuing to use this system					
	1	2	3	4	5

What are your thoughts on this tool/suggestion?

Thank you for taking part in this survey.

Appendix C - Online Questionnaire Template

Questionnaire for health professionals

Research for a design course completion project at UFPE to find out how technology, aimed at scheduling and registering patients, is present in the daily lives of healthcare professionals.

1. Profession *

( )Doctor

( )Nutritionist

( )Physiotherapist

( )Dentist

( )Other:

2. How many years have you been working in the field? *

( )less than 1 year

( )1--5 years

( )6--10 years

( )11-20 years

( )more than 20 years

3. Where do you work? * Office

( )Clinic

( )Hospital

( )Other:

4. Do you have your own clinic/consultancy/hospital? Which one(s)? *

---

5. What tool do you use to schedule your patients? *

( )Paper diary

( )Agenda organizing website

( )Mobile applications

( )Desktop systems

( )Other:

6. If you use a digital tool to schedule patients, which one(s) would it be?

7. How do you register your patients? *

8. How is the appointment confirmed with the patient? *

MIX
Papier aus verantwortungsvollen Quellen
Paper from responsible sources
FSC® C105338

Printed by Books on Demand GmbH, Norderstedt / Germany